IMAGES
of America

SINGER CASTLE
REVISITED

Singer Castle, the first book written by Robert and Patty Mondore about the castle on Dark Island, was completed in 2003. *Singer Castle Revisited* picks up where the story left off. It will not only describe the extensive renovations the castle has undergone but will also take a look back at some of its previously unrecorded details. This picture was taken shortly after it was purchased by Dark Island Tours, Inc. in 2002. (Authors' collection.)

ON THE COVER: The cover photograph is a breathtaking aerial view of Singer Castle taken around the time it was purchased by its new owners. (Farhad Vladi.)

IMAGES
of America

SINGER CASTLE
REVISITED

Robert and Patty Mondore

ARCADIA
PUBLISHING

Copyright © 2010 by Robert and Patty Mondore
ISBN 978-0-7385-7302-1

Published by Arcadia Publishing
Charleston, South Carolina

Printed in the United States of America

Library of Congress Control Number: 2009940372

For all general information contact Arcadia Publishing at:
Telephone 843-853-2070
Fax 843-853-0044
E-mail sales@arcadiapublishing.com
For customer service and orders:
Toll-Free 1-888-313-2665

Visit us on the Internet at www.arcadiapublishing.com

*To Ken Hard and Ralph Berry. It is because of your generosity
that* Singer Castle Revisited *could come to be.*

CONTENTS

ACKNOWLEDGMENTS

There are several reasons we were able to revisit Singer Castle. We would probably not have even thought of doing a second book if it were not for the inspiration of one of the castle's owners, Farhad Vladi. He felt that there was more to tell of the wonderful story of the castle on Dark Island, especially now that so much additional time, work, and money have been invested into making it the treasure of the Thousand Islands that it is today. But just as importantly, it is because of the generosity of Ken Hard (grandson of Frederick Bourne) and Ralph Berry (nephew of Dr. Harold Martin) in sharing their cherished family photographs with us. We that hope what we have written gives due honor to the Bourne and Martin families. In addition, we are extremely indebted to the team at Singer Castle who shared their time, their talents, and their vast knowledge with us. We are so grateful to Tom Weldon, the president of Singer Castle; Judy Keeler, the castle historian (among other talents); and Scott Garris, the year-round caretaker and island photographer, for all of their help and for their willingness to so freely share all of the information that they had with us. And of course we thank Harvey and Flo Jones for their help and for sharing their stories with us.

Unless otherwise noted, all images appear courtesy of the authors. A large percentage of the remaining photographs appear courtesy of Kenneth Hard (KH), grandson of Frederick Bourne; Farhad Vladi (FV), one of the present owners; or Ralph Berry (RB), nephew of Harold Martin. In addition, we received several of the Bourne family photographs courtesy of Judy Keeler (JK), the Singer Castle historian. We are indebted to all of these individuals for their help.

INTRODUCTION

Much has happened since our first book, *Singer Castle*, was released in 2005. In fact, the castle purchased in 2002 is in many ways almost a brand-new castle, thanks to the investments of time, labor, and money that Dark Island Tours, Inc. has poured into it. In addition to the many marvelous renovations that have taken place, *Singer Castle* had barely come off the press when we started receiving all kinds of previously unseen historical photographs, facts, historical anecdotes, and details from gracious family members willing to share their collections with us. Between the updates on the castle as well as the new information on its fascinating "three-castle" history, we felt all of this necessitated a second volume, taking the reader on a revisit with us to our beloved castle on Dark Island.

This book will not attempt to repeat the history and details available in the first book. To briefly bring the reader up to date, Singer Castle is a magnificent 28-room castle, complete with turrets, secret passageways, and even a dungeon. Completed in 1905 for its first owner, Frederick G. Bourne, it is located in heart of the Thousand Islands in Upstate New York. Bourne was the president of the Singer Manufacturing Company, through which he became one of the wealthiest men in the world. He was the consummate businessman, but also had plenty of time for hobbies and recreation, which included summer visits to the Thousand Islands. When he decided to purchase one of those islands for himself and have a "hunting lodge" built on it, he contacted his friend and world-renowned architect, Ernest Flagg, to design it for him. At the time, Flagg was reading Sir Walter Scott's historical novel, *Woodstock* (1826), which was written around a fictionalized but historic castle. This would be the model Flagg used for what Bourne would later refer to as "The Towers" on Dark Island.

The family enjoyed the castle for the next 14 years, until Bourne's death in 1919. After his death, two of his daughters—May Strassburger and Marjorie Bourne—purchased the castle. In 1921, May gave lifetime use of the castle to Marjorie. Marjorie married Alexander Thayer in 1926 and the couple spent the next 35 summers there at the castle. Marjorie passed away in 1962, after deeding the castle to LaSalle Christian brothers, who sold it to the Harold Martin Evangelistic Association in 1965. Dr. Martin renamed the castle "Jorstadt Castle" after his grandfather, who was a Norwegian sea captain. Opening the castle doors to the public for the first time, the Martins used the castle for spiritual retreats and Sunday chapel services, which were continued even after Dr. Martin's death in 1999. (Eloise Martin died in 2004.) In 2002, the castle was purchased and its name changed to Singer Castle by its three present owners, who make up the investment group Dark Island Tours, Inc.

With each of its name changes, the castle has taken on a different character and has taken its own distinct place in history. It was named Singer Castle by its current owners because this magnificent edifice was built through the wealth Commodore Bourne gained from the Singer Manufacturing

Company. However, without having to look very far, one could also find a recurring theme of music—particularly singers—throughout all three of its histories.

The history of the castle on Dark Island proves wealth coupled with generosity makes for some of the best possible kinds of blessings. This is, of course, especially true for the many recipients of unanticipated gifts and acts of kindness, but also for everyone who is encouraged by such a generous spirit to do the same. Frederick G. Bourne was one of the wealthiest men in the world, and was well known for giving extremely large portions of his wealth to charitable causes. Commodore Bourne's daughter Marjorie, like her father, was also known for being a generous and giving person. The Martins, though not considered wealthy, were known for being generous with what they had. Over the years they owned the castle, they spent much of the money they did have in maintaining the castle even when they were no longer able to go there, so that the castle and its chapel services could remain open to the public. They wanted to share with others the one thing that was more precious to them than anything else—their faith in God. Well into their 80s they worked throughout the winter months to be able to afford the many bills and repair costs needed to keep the castle's doors open during the summer.

In keeping with the castle's more than 100-year tradition, Dark Island Tours, Inc. has used its investors' wealth to invest in the castle on Dark Island, in part, to bring this lovely historical landmark back to its original pristine condition and to continue to make it available for the public to enjoy. Their costs to date, above and beyond the original purchase price, are quickly pressing towards $10 million. But their generosity has once again opened the doors of this unique piece of Thousand Islands history for the world to see and enjoy, and to experience for themselves. It is also because of the generosity of members of the Bourne and Martin families and the staff at Singer Castle that this book could record the people and the history that brought the castle to what it is today—a magnificent structure that is a testimony to character and generosity.

This volume will revisit the castle's rich history as we share some of the wonderful historical pictures we have received from family members and other sources. We will end by giving the reader a tour of the new Singer Castle, as it appears today. But don't just take our word for it. The castle's doors remain open throughout the summer, inviting you to come and tour it in person for yourself.

One

THE TOWERS
THE CASTLE BUILT BY A SINGER

In 1902, Frederick Bourne, president of the Singer Manufacturing Company, decided to purchase a 7-acre island in the Thousand Island region, where he would build what he fondly referred to as a hunting lodge. Two years later, his "hunting lodge," modeled after the castle in Sir Walter Scott's historical novel *Woodstock*, was complete. He named his castle The Towers after the castle in the story.

Frederick G. Bourne was the son of Harriet Gilbert and Rev. George Washington Bourne (pictured here). Reverend Bourne was a humble preacher from New England, who moved his family to New York City when Frederick and his two sisters, May Louise and Clara, and his brother, William Theodore, were children. Frederick Bourne would one day become the president of one of the largest and most successful international conglomerates of his day. (KH.)

Dark Island Tours, Inc. named Singer Castle based upon the wealth Bourne earned from the sewing machine. Interestingly, Frederick Bourne, who probably never even met his company's founder, Isaac Singer, was an excellent singer with a beautiful baritone voice. He got his first job at the Singer Company in part because he sang in the same choir as Alfred Clark, whose father was the president of Singer Manufacturing Company.

Frederick G. Bourne (1851–1919) earned his fortune by taking the Singer Manufacturing Company to its international success. He also was involved in several other businesses, including the Aeolian Company, Atlas Portland Cement, Knickerbocker Safe Deposit, Long Island Motor Parkway, Long Island Railroad, and Bank of Manhattan (to name a few), all of which contributed to making him one of the wealthiest men in the world. Bourne was known throughout his life to be an extremely kindhearted and generous man. (KH.)

Frederick Bourne married Emma Keeler (1855–1916), on February 9, 1875. Emma was the daughter of James Rufus and Mary Louise Davison Keeler, a longtime New York family, and a granddaughter of Commodore Davidson, one of the founders of the New York Yacht Club. (KH.)

Within the first 18 years of their marriage, Frederick and Emma celebrated the births of 12 children: Frederick, Arthur, Louisa, May, Marion, Alfred, Helen, Florence, George, Marjorie, Kenneth, and Howard. Frederick, Louisa, Helen, and Kenneth all died as children. Howard died just one year before his father. The other seven married, and five of the couples had children, some of whom are living today. (KH.)

Despite all of his business and recreational involvements, Frederick Bourne was first and foremost a devoted family man who deeply loved his wife, children, and, as pictured above, eventually grandchildren. While Bourne would leave a great deal of money to charities, the largest portion of his wealth would eventually be left to his seven living children. (KH.)

Pictured here are the following members of the Bourne family, from left to right: (first row) Anson Hard (husband of Florence Bourne), Kenneth Bourne (son of Alfred), Arthur Bourne Jr, Alfred Bourne (son of Arthur), and Howard Bourne; (second row) Florence Bourne Hard with her children George and Frederick, and Louise Barnes (wife of Alfred) holding daughter Barbara; (third row) Arthur Bourne and wife Ethel Hollins, George Bourne and wife Helen Whitney, Marjorie, Frederick and Emma Bourne, Ralph Strassburger and wife May Bourne, and Alfred and Marion Bourne. (KH.)

Along with his expanding family, Bourne was also expanding his real estate, which included the family estate in Oakdale. Indian Neck Hall was completed in early 1900, just in time for their 25th wedding anniversary. Designed by Ernest Flagg (who would also later design the Singer Tower for Bourne), this palatial estate was 300 feet long by 125 feet deep, and contained about 100 rooms. (KH.)

In addition to his many business interests, Bourne was also an avid sportsman with many interests and hobbies, including hunting, fishing, boxing, horses, and boats. He also loved motorcars. He was one of the first in the area to own an automobile and was a skilled driver. He imported a number of European cars, including a $10,000 Mercedes. In today's currency that would be approximately $254,000. (KH.)

Along with fast cars, Bourne enjoyed fast horses. Among his prize-winning horses were Enthorpe, Performer, Starlight, Princess Olga, Indian Queen, Priscilla, Tomahawk, Jennie Neils, and His Grace. (KH.)

For several years Bourne devoted a great deal of time and money to raising horses at his stables in Oakdale. In the late 1890s, he brought home many ribbons from the National Horse Shows in New York, as well as from shows in Boston and Philadelphia. (KH.)

But without a doubt, Frederick Bourne's favorite hobby was boating. He owned boats of all shapes, sizes, makes, and motors. The first yacht he acquired was the *Maria*, which he purchased in England in 1902, and renamed the *Delaware*. He was a member of several yacht clubs, including the prestigious New York Yacht Club, where he was named commodore from 1903–1905. (KH.)

The *Delaware* was a 253-foot screw schooner designed by G. L. Watson and built by Napier, Shanks, and Bell in 1896. Bourne owned it from 1903–1905, and had a crew of over 100. He used it as the flagship for the New York Yacht Club (NYYC) while he was commodore. It burned at Hoboken in 1905, and was sold, restored, and used again by another owner as the flagship of the NYYC. Today the bell from the *Delaware* still hangs on the clock tower at Singer Castle. (KH.)

It was primarily his interest in boating that brought Frederick Bourne to the Thousand Islands. George Boldt was building his Thousand Islands castle at the time Bourne became a member of Thousand Islands Yacht Club. The Bournes and the Boldts were acquainted, and in fact, Frederick Bourne would one day be a pallbearer at George Boldt's funeral.

Eventually Bourne decided to purchase one of the islands for himself. Dark Island was part of a 35-mile tract of islands purchased for $3,000 in 1845 by Azariah Walton of Alexandria Bay, New York. In October 1891, the island was sold for $200 to William Harison. Formerly known as Bluff, Lone Star, or Dark Island, it was sold for $5,000 to Frederick Bourne by William Harison, his wife, Mary Francis, and Noble Wymberly Harison, December 3, 1902. (KH.)

Construction began in October 1903 by the J. B. and R. I. Reid Construction Company of Alexandria Bay. A June 1905 census report in the town of Hammond stated that there were 116 men on the payroll. The men lived in a floating rooming house constructed on a large scow tied to the island. (KH.)

The castle was designed by world-renowned architect and Bourne's personal friend, Ernest M. Flagg. In addition to Indian Neck Hall, Flagg designed St. Luke's Hospital and the Scribner Building in New York City, several buildings at the U.S. Naval Academy in Maryland, the Corcoran Gallery of Art in Washington, D.C., and eventually the Singer Building, also in New York City, which was temporarily the tallest building in the world.

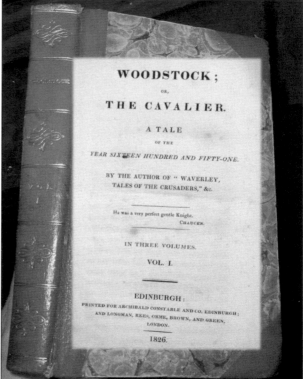

Flagg enjoyed having his wife read stories to him every evening at 7:00 p.m. At the time Bourne requested his hunting lodge, they were reading Sir Walter Scott's *Woodstock*. So Flagg patterned Bourne's hunting lodge after the mysterious castle where, in Scott's novel, King Charles II hid from Sir Oliver Cromwell. Pictured here is an 1826 first edition of *Woodstock* that was recently donated to Singer Castle.

Ernest Flagg's original blueprints from May 1903 show the castle the way it was originally designed and built. Bourne, and later his daughter Marjorie, would make several changes and additions to the original building. What is now the library on the ground floor was originally a billiard room. (RB.)

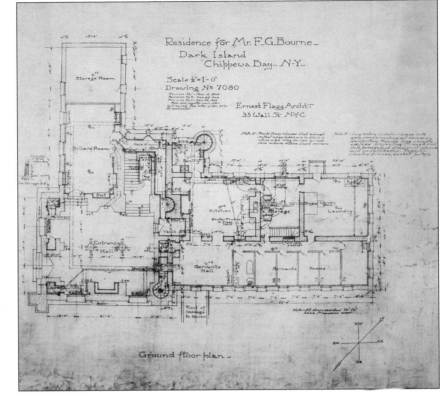

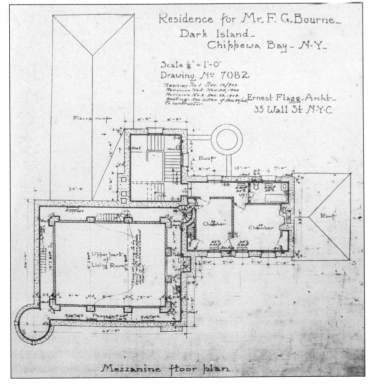

The mezzanine blueprints give a good look at one of the main secret passageways that circumnavigate the trophy room. One can also notice the original design for the breakfast room, which was later replaced by the much larger breakfast room found in the castle today. The piazza was later divided into two separate rooms, with a second floor added above it as living quarters for the owners. (RB.)

Construction by the J. B. and R. L. Reid Construction Company of Alexandria Bay began in the spring of 1903. Granite was quarried from Oak Island and sandstone from Hammond. For the next two years, the construction continued year-round. In the winter, lumber and stone were ferried from the mainland by wagons over the ice. The castle would initially contain 28 rooms in addition to eight fireplaces and eight and a half bathrooms, located on six different levels. The castle has three towers: the front tower/turret, the conical tower that contains the water tower, and the tower in back with the butler pantry (pictured on the right side in the left image). (Both, RB.)

The castle was completed in 1905. It has been estimated that to duplicate such an architectural wonder today would cost well over $40 million. But Bourne would soon begin all kinds of additional changes and renovations on his Towers. It was rumored that as the castle neared its original completion, Bourne asked designer Ernest Flagg if he had any regrets. Flagg responded, "Only that I didn't build a similar one for myself." (KH.)

Pictured is the living room, as it was referred to in the original designs. It has also been referred to as the trophy room, for obvious reasons. The walls were adorned with a variety of game trophies most likely taken by Bourne, who was an avid hunter, and made the castle quite legitimately his hunting lodge. (KH.)

The dining room, located just off the trophy room, featured (still to this day) an A. J. Horner table with its legs adorned by griffins. (KH.)

Just off the dining room was the cozy little single-story wooden breakfast room with awnings on its windows. It was approximately 19 feet by 14 feet. This room would later be replaced by a much larger breakfast room and terrace. (KH.)

On the ground floor just off of the great hall was the billiard room. To the left of the fireplace, one of the panels could mysteriously be opened up and was an entrance to one of many secret passageways. (KH.)

The first impression Bourne's guests would have after entering the massive wooden doors was the great hall. It was formed with massive stone arches, infinity mirrors, medieval weaponry, and even three suites of medieval armor Bourne had purchased for his castle. (KH.)

From the great hall, the wide granite staircase with carved wooden balustrades leads to the first floor, where the living room, dining room, breakfast room, and piazza were located. (KH.)

The original design called for a large single-roomed piazza or patio located just off of the living room. It was comprised of windows on three sides with a panoramic view of the river and overlooked the back lawn and tennis courts. The Bournes decorated this room with wicker furniture, and it was therefore referred to as the wicker room or the sunroom. (KH.)

From the south boathouse one could enter the castle either by ascending the stone bridle path or via a staircase located in the connected four-story tower. In fact, the tower entrance was part of a complete passageway system that led to the castle and also over to the north boathouse. The bell on the tower (which is still there today) was the bell from Bourne's steam yacht, the *Delaware*. (KH.)

The day finally arrived when Bourne brought his family out to see, for the first time, the "hunting lodge" he had been telling them about. One can only imagine their surprise when they came around the islands outside of Chippewa Bay that hid Bourne's Towers from view. (KH.)

It apparently didn't take too long for the Bourne family to get over any initial surprise. Pictured are Frederick Bourne (second from right) and some of his family getting ready for a dip off the main dock. (KH.)

Bourne also purchased several neighboring islands—Corn, Cordwood, Marsh, and Ice Islands—from which he brought over 2,000 loads of topsoil to Dark Island. He also used the islands for vegetable gardening and duck hunting (note the castle in the background). On one particularly successful excursion, Bourne wrote a note to his children letting them know they had gotten 84 ducks that day and that it was a "Good day for us; bad day for the ducks." (KH.)

George Waldo Browne, in his 1905 book, *The Saint Lawrence River*, wrote about an island fortress called La Presentation—the lone French stronghold that was ultimately destroyed in the French and Indian War. This island was plainly visible from Dark Island. Frederick Bourne acquired an interest in the island, which he later sold. But before he did, he had the chimney repaired. This picture was taken from the Canadian shore looking out at Chimney Island with the castle in the background.

Two

THE TOWERS:
THE BOURNES' BUILDINGS, BOATS, AND OBITS

Between the time his Towers were first completed and his death in 1919, Frederick Bourne had several additions and changes made to the castle's original design. This chapter opens with descriptions of those additions as well as some of the additions he made to his collection of yachts and speedboats. This chapter ends with a look at some of tributes to Frederick Bourne made by the many people who loved and admired him.

In 1910, Frederick Bourne decided to have another 40 feet added to the north boathouse bringing it to 125 feet to be able to accommodate a 100-foot steam yacht. He also added a dam on the end for a dry dock with screw jacks to raise the yacht from the water for winter storage. Shown here is the north boathouse as it was originally built.

Early in 1910, a crew of 37 men worked around the clock on the north boathouse, adding the 40-foot-long, one-story addition that moved the location of the power plant and included additional living quarters for servants. An area 90 feet long, 26 feet wide, and 12.5 feet deep was blasted out of the rock to increase the size of the dockage for Bourne's new 111-foot steam yacht, the *Sioux*. (RB.)

Here is the north boathouse as it appears today, with the added 40 feet in length and the second-story servants' quarters. Restoring the north boathouse to its original condition is one of the projects being planned by its current owners. (RB.)

The current caretaker's cottage was originally used as an icehouse. Sometime around 1911, Bourne added a new icehouse on the northern side of the island. Pictured are the work teams cutting and loading ice into the nearly completed icehouse in the background (note the breakfast room addition had already been added). (KH.)

During this same time period, the small wooden breakfast room off the dining room, pictured above, was removed. It was replaced by a new two-story wing with a larger breakfast room and an expanded suite of bedrooms above it. (KH.)

The new 19-foot-by-39-foot breakfast room was about three times larger than the former building and would be used for entertaining guests. It would later become a chapel. The expanded upper suite of rooms is used today as the Royal Suites for overnight visitors. (RB.)

Also sometime between 1911 and 1916, a fifth floor and large clock with four clock faces, each 6 feet in diameter, were added to the south boathouse tower. Pictured is the four-story tower prior to the addition. (RB.)

The clock was made by E. Howard Clocks and had Westminster chimes that would sound every 15 minutes. It is a self-regulating clock that works by weights. A motor was added to wind the clock by pulling the weights. This magnificent clock is valued today at over $75,000. Still operational, its chimes continue to sound on the quarter-hour today. (KH.)

DARK ISLAND ST. LAWRENCE RIVER RESIDENCE OF COMMODORE BOURNE, N.Y.C.

Bourne also added another inside slip to the south boathouse sometime between 1911 and 1916. Pictured are two different views of the original south boathouse when it still had only two inside and two outside slips.

This series of pictures shows multiple views of the various stages of construction as the additional slip is being added to the south boathouse. One can also note the four-story tower in the background, showing that the addition to the boathouse predates the addition of the fifth-floor clock tower. (KH.)

This picture shows all of the additions and work completed during Frederick Bourne's lifetime, including the added slip to the south boathouse, the clock tower, and the larger breakfast room.

Here is a picture taken from the inside of the south boathouse shortly after it was completed. It apparently didn't take Frederick Bourne too long to fill his expanded boathouse with boats. (KH.)

It shouldn't be a surprise that Bourne added to both of his island boathouses. He owned an extraordinary collection of yachts and speedboats, many of which he kept at the Towers. Pictured is one of his speedboats with Corn Island (which he also owned) in the background. (KH.)

His better-known yachts were the *Delaware*, the *Colonia*, and the *Artemis*. The largest, and perhaps most impressive, was the *Alberta*, designed by G. L. Watson and built by the Ailsa Shipbuilding Company in 1896. It was a 278-foot screw steam, twin schooner requiring a crew of 55 that Bourne owned from 1915–1917. The *Alberta* was chartered by explorer Alexander Hamilton Rice in 1916 for one of his South American expeditions. (KH.)

COLONIA	GARDNER & COX	DELAWARE RIVER IRON SHIPPING	SCREW SCHOONER	1899	189 LOA	EX ALBERTA, FGB 1901-1909
CONSTITUTION	N.G. HERRESHOFF	HERRESHOFF MFG.	SLOOP	1901	90 LWL	FGB SYNDICATE MEMBER 1901-1905
REVERIE	G.M. SMITH	G.M. SMITH	CB SLOOP	1901	48 LOA	FGB 1902-1907
DELAWARE	G.L. WATSON	NAPIER, SHANKS, BELL	SCREW SCHOONER	1896	253 LOA	EX MARIA, FGB 1903-1905
SCAT	GARDNER & COX	SAMUEL AYERS	SCREW STEAM	1902	70 LOA	FGB 1903-1916
MERIAM	G.M. SMITH	G.M. SMITH	CB CAT	1899	26'6 LOA	FGB 1904-1909
CANVASBACK	N.G. HERRESHOFF	HERRESHOFF MFG.	K TC SCWL	1909	59 LOA	FGB 1909-1916
SIOUX	N.G. HERRESHOFF	HERRESHOFF MFG.	K TC SC STEAM	1904	111 LOA	EX LITTLE SOVEREIGN I, FGB 1910-1919
DARK ISLAND	C.L. SEABURY	GAS ENGINE & POWER	K TC SCW STEAM	1912	60 LOA	FGB 1912-1919
ALBERTA	G.L. WATSON	AILSA SHIPBUILDING	SCW STEAM, TW SCHOONER	1896	278 LOA	EX MARGARITA, FGB 1915-1917
JOAN III	H.J. GIELOW	W.F. DOWNS	CD TC AUX YAWL	1906	55 LOA	FGB 1919

*AS TAKEN FROM AMERICAN YACHT REGISTRIES
LIST COMPILED BY LINDSEY TOTINO, CURATOR, NEW YORK YACHT CLUB, 2009

This list of boats registered to Frederick Bourne was compiled by Lindsey Totino, curator of the New York Yacht Club, for a NYYC exhibit on Frederick Bourne in January 2010. Bourne owned numerous additional smaller boats that would not have needed to be registered. (JK.)

The *Dark Island* was a 60-foot yacht built for Frederick Bourne by the Gas Engine and Power Company and Charles L. Seabury and Company in 1912. It was one of the early fast day yachts with gasoline power and attained a speed of about 20 miles per hour. Ownership would later be transferred to Marjorie Bourne in 1923, and then to her husband, Alexander Thayer, in 1929. (KH.)

Frederick and later Marjorie Bourne entered their boats in several of the many speedboat races held in the St. Lawrence River. Frederick competed in the Gold Cup Races that were held there between 1905 and 1913. They competed against some of the fastest boats in the world. This picture includes the Gold Cup winner, *Dixie II* (bottom left), and the Bournes' *Moike* (bottom right). Bourne would have also entered his speedboat the *Messenger* and might very well have won over the *Dixie* had the 50-foot-long boat not been 10 feet longer than allowed. (KH.)

Both Frederick and Marjorie Bourne won several of the speedboat races they competed in. In 1907, Frederick's boat *Stranger* took the Frontenac cup. In fact, the fireplace mantel in the Towers' trophy room was covered with trophies Bourne had won (see page 23). Several of the trophies won by Frederick and Marjorie are now on display at the Antique Boat Museum in Clayton.

Not all of Bourne's boats were speedboats or steam yachts. This picture is of the small skiff house located at the eastern end of the island. The skiff house later had a pulley system and drop down floor added, and it was large enough to house quite a number of boats. (KH.)

There were also boats that were neither fast nor practical. Bourne and his family enjoyed cruising around the islands in his electric gondola. It is likely the only electric gondola ever to cruise the Thousand Islands. (KH.)

Frederick and Emma Bourne, often accompanied by some of their eight surviving children and their families, enjoyed their Towers on Dark Island from the time of its completion in 1905 until Emma's death on August 31, 1916. The *Suffolk County News* published the tribute below. (KH.)

"Mrs. Bourne . . . was devoted to her husband, her family, and her home. For many years, she had given much of her time and thought and abundant means to charitable work . . . Of this the general public learned almost nothing, but the many who in time of trouble have known her kindly helping hand will join with the family in mourning sincerely the passing of a good woman who was much beloved." (KH.)

BUSINESS AMERICA

MAY 1914

ANOTHER GREAT PHILANTHROPIST

The portrait of Frederick Gilbert Bourne, ex-Commodore of the New York Yacht Club, painted two years ago by George R. Boynton, the celebrated portrait painter, reflects the qualities of character which made possible his magnificent gift of $500,000 to the Choral School of the Cathedral of St. John the Divine. None familiar with the engaging complexities of his nature, his genius for business and his unaffected piety, his geniality in his clubs and his domesticity in his home, his interest in art, in letters and in sports, wondered that his full, rich and abundant sympathies found one form of expression in this characteristic munificence. The only condition he attached to its acceptance was his election as a member of the choir! He has long been in choirs—as boy and man.

Dr. Ludwig Fulda, in a recent interview, on leaving America for his home in Germany, described the American people not as materialists but as idealists, and our millionaires as first of all philanthropists. He referred to the enormous sums given to education, social service, research, religion and experiment as expressing not only the impulse of the individual but the essential national quality of the people. Commodore Bourne's Easter offering had not, at that time, transpired, and it is easy to believe that Dr. Fulda's knowledge of it will enlarge his impressions by the purely esthetic and spiritual value of the Bourne endowment. The Choral School is worthy the distinction. The choir, under the direction of Dr. Miles Farrow, the organist of the Cathedral, is already the best in this country,

Frederick Bourne died in 1919. He has been an extremely generous man throughout his life and was no less generous in his death—leaving over $350,000 (about $43 million in today's currency) to various churches and charitable organizations. *Business America* described: "The qualities of character which made possible his magnificent gift of $500,000 to the Choral School of the Cathedral of St. John the Divine. None familiar with the engaging complexities of his nature, his genius for business and his unaffected piety, his geniality in his clubs and his domesticity in his home . . . wondered that his full, rich, and abundant sympathies found one form of expression in this characteristic munificence."

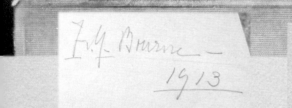

F. G. Bourne —
1913

as long as the longest road. God's love is
as long as the longest day. God's love is as
long as the longest night. God's love is as
long as life. God's love is as long as eternity.
" I have loved thee with an everlasting love."
' I will never leave thee *nor* forsake thee."
' Love never faileth."

price." But for that pearl we may have to
sell many others. What are we prepared to
give for it? What are we ready to surren-
der? According to our consecrated enterprise
will be our holy gains. If we refuse to par
with Mammon we can never possess the Lord
If we contentedly hug the good we can neve
gain the better. If we take our ease in th
realm of the better we can never enter the bes
What are we ready to lose for Christ?

> Were the whole realm of nature mine,
> That were an offering far too small.
> Love so amazing, so divine,
> Demands my life, my soul, my all.

The Long Island Railroad Company wrote: "Combining fidelity and trust with a rare business ability he commanded respect, while his lovable personality gained for him the genuine affection of all with whom he came into close contact." One might wonder what made a man like Frederick Bourne tick. Perhaps one clue could be found in what he read—even more in what he marked and highlighted. This book, *Things That Matter Most*, by world-renowned preacher J. H. Jowett, with marks handwritten by Bourne remains in the castle library today.

Three

THE TOWERS
THE MARJORIE BOURNE YEARS

DARK ISLAND, THOUSAND ISLANDS, N. Y. MARJORIE BOURNE RESIDENCE. 23822

Frederick Bourne's youngest daughter, Marjorie Bourne, would spend the next 43 years enjoying Bourne's Towers. Of all the individuals who have owned the castle throughout its history, Marjorie owned it for the longest period of time. (KH.)

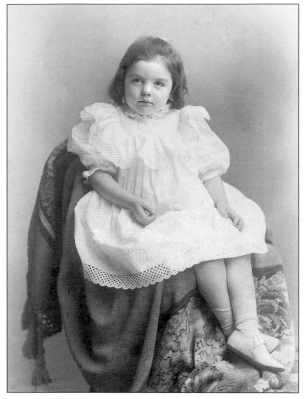

After their father's death, Marjorie (pictured above at four years old) and her older sister May (Bourne) Strassburger purchased the castle from the family estate at a cost of $389,000. In 1921, May gave lifetime use of the castle to Marjorie. The two sisters remained close throughout their lives. (KH.)

Pictured is May Bourne when she was 12 years old. May was Marjorie's oldest sister (the two were nine years apart in age). May married Ralph Beaver Strassburger (publisher and newspaper owner) in 1911, and they spent their time between their estate in Pennsylvania (Normandy Farms) and their villa in France, where Marjorie occasionally went to visit them. (KH.)

Pictured is Marjorie Bourne (1890–1962), who was fondly referred to as "Hooley" by her friends and family. This picture was taken in 1926 upon her arrival back in the United States after visiting May and her husband in Europe. (Underwood and Underwood Glass Stereograph Collection, Archives Center, National Museum of American History, Smithsonian Institution.)

Marjorie also remained close to several of her other siblings and their families, including George, Howard, and her other sisters. She was especially close to her sister Florence, pictured above at 18 years of age. Florence, who married Anson Hard, was four years older than Marjorie, and the closest sister to her in age. (KH.)

Florence asked Marjorie to be godmother to her daughter and namesake, Florence Bourne Hard, who was born in 1925. Young Florence was said to have described days she spent with her Aunt Hooley as "never a dull moment." (KH.)

In 1910, Marjorie attempted to race a train in her automobile. The 5-mile race was between Islip and Oakdale, and the train beat her by only a few feet. The *New York Times* noted that "it has been said that it has long been the ambition of each one of [the Bournes] to return home some night and tell of having beaten the express into Oakdale" and that young Marjorie would likely "repeat the attempt until she succeeds." (George G. Ayling Collection, David Keller Archive).

Lawrnce, Long Island, N. Y.,

August 31, 1911.

The bearer, Mrs. Florence B. Hard, wife of Mr. Anson W. Hard, Jr., is hereby licensed to own or carry six revolvers or pistols, six rifles and six shotguns. This license shall be good until revoked.

POLICE JUSTICE,
VILLAGE OF LAWRENCE,
NASSAU COUNTY, N. Y.

Not a typical society girl, Marjorie, like both her mother and father, enjoyed shooting and hunting. The Bourne family enjoyed hunting and owned many guns (legally, of course). Pictured is a copy of Florence (Bourne) Hard's gun permit. Gun laws were less restrictive back then than they are today. (KH.)

Emma Bourne (pictured here) enjoyed hunting ducks perhaps just as much as her husband did. Marjorie and some of her other siblings would eventually follow suit. In 1923, the Hammond paper reported that Marjorie came up to the island with 15 friends to go duck hunting. After her father's death, Marjorie retained two-thirds interest in Ice Island for the express purpose of shooting ducks there. (Kathy Mooney.)

Marjorie was an accomplished shooter. In fact the *Sporting News* recorded in December 1909 that "[Marjorie] won a shooting match the other day, shooting three pheasants out of five. The women are coming on." (KH.)

Marjorie purchased her parents' cottage at the prestigious Jekyll Island Club in Georgia from the Strassburgers in 1923. Frederick Bourne had been president of the Jekyll Island Club from 1914–1919. A Tiffany stained-glass window in Jekyll Island's Faith Chapel was dedicated to her father's memory, with one of the inscriptions saying, "I will sing unto the Lord, for He has triumphed gloriously." (KH.)

Marjorie spent many of her childhood winters on Jekyll Island with her family. Pictured is Marjorie with her youngest brother, Howard, who had health problems throughout his life and died the year before his father. Some felt the loss of both son and wife contributed to Frederick Bourne's own relatively early death. (KH.)

Marjorie was also a member of the Thousand Islands Club, where she enjoyed playing and competing in tennis matches. She was a friend and competitor of George Boldt's daughter, Clover, who also enjoyed tennis and speedboats. The two women played and raced in many of the same contests. Marjorie could practice, of course, right on her own courts on Dark Island (KH.)

In an August 2, 1921, article titled "Tennis Matches Start at River," the *Watertown Times* reported on the annual tennis tournament at the Thousand Islands Yacht Club, where Marjorie was listed as a competitor in the women's singles. Her brother-in-law Ralph Strassburger (May's husband) competed in the men's doubles along with Clover's husband, A. G. Miles. (KH.)

54

Like her father, Marjorie also had a passion for fast boats. Pictured is Marjorie in the 37-foot speedboat her father purchased for her 16th birthday in 1906, from J. B. Ried. Originally named *Eureka*, Marjorie changed the name to *Moike*. In 1910, she entered and captained the *Moike* in a race beating several former Gold Cup winners. A *New York Times* headline reported, "New York Girl Steers a Motor Boat to Victory," having "the fastest motorboat of the Thousand Islands." (KI I.)

Marjorie had her own share of trophies, and several of them are displayed today alongside her father's trophies at the Antique Boat Museum in Clayton. The *Moike* itself now also belongs to the museum and is on display there. (See page 42.)

Marjorie was also known for her generosity and charitable giving. The 1912 *New York Times* recorded one of her annual Christmas parties in West Sayville, where she gave out gifts to each of some 300 children. It was reported that she "gladdened the hearts of all of the children in the village today by playing the role of Santa Claus for them." (Pictured is the Indian Neck Hall family estate in West Sayville). (KH.)

It is unclear when the castle billiard room was converted to a library. Marjorie may have done this in 1923, since she placed a large order that year for books to be shipped to Dark Island. She also had custom bookplates made that are still in many of the library's volumes today. Marjorie kept most, if not all, of her father's Jowett books (see page 46), some of which she herself had originally given to him.

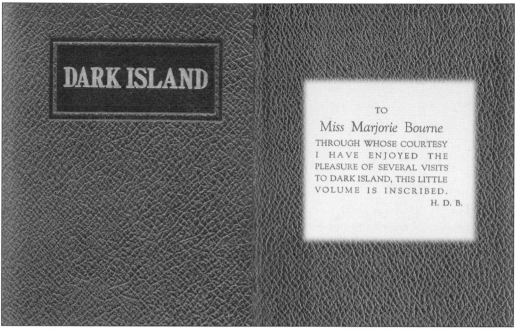

It was well known that Marjorie was socially involved wherever she went. And she loved to open the doors of her Towers to share with family and friends. One of the yet-unsolved castle mysteries is a small, black leather-bound book simply called *Dark Island* that was printed (in an unknown quantity) sometime between 1921 and 1926 as a thank-you gift to Marjorie Bourne for a writer only identified by the initials H. D. B.

The book gave a brief history of the castle, the region, and the life of Frederick Bourne. There are a few original few copies of *Dark Island* still in existence today, and Singer Castle has an original copy on display. The castle has printed a new edition of the book so guests today can purchase their own copy of this unique and historical keepsake souvenir.

Marjorie also had sets of color postcards printed, and she apparently included a set inside each copy of *Dark Island*. This postcard shows the breakfast room. Constructed with stone and walnut, the room is bright and open, having large Gothic windows on three sides. It was, no doubt, the room where Marjorie and her guests would share meals and enjoy both the sunrises and sunsets. (Below, KH.)

MAIN ENTRANCE, THE TOWERS

The great hall is the first view that the guests would see. It was the perfect scene for creating the ambience of a historical castle. Measuring 39 feet by 33 feet, this magnificent entryway has massive pillars, beautifully carved stone arched walls, and ceilings crafted by Italian masons. It was appropriately decorated with medieval armor and antiques. (Below, KH.)

BOAT HOUSE AND DOCK, THE TOWERS

This view of the south boathouse was taken from about halfway down the bridle path looking east toward Ogdensburg (or Brockville). Pictured is the 60-foot *Dark Island*, waiting in the same place where it had so often been docked at the time of Frederick Bourne. (Below, KH.)

INDIAN WALK, THE TOWERS

The lovely Indian Walk winds around the western point of the island to a protected bathing area. It is unclear why the trail was given this name, but several tribes of Native Americans (Algonquin, Huron, and Iroquois) had once inhabited this area. Various arrowheads and relics were later discovered on the island, including a granite grinding stone that remains there today. (Below, KH.)

VIEW FROM DOCK, THE TOWERS

This view from the dock looks up the winding bridle path to the main entrance of the castle. About halfway up the path there is a turret-styled stone sitting area with a beautiful view of the river. Just below the path, Frederick Bourne had an ornamental cannon, which points to the United States rather than Canada, to avoid potential international tensions. (Below, KH.)

This is a view of the castle arriving from the southeast. The additions of the added slip, breakfast room, and clock tower at visible in this postcard view.

Marjorie made sure that any postcard collection she gave out included a picture of the back of the castle, along with an excellent view of the tennis courts. This photograph was taken before she later added a third-story addition.

UPPER LOGGIA, THE TOWERS

This postcard is a picture of the loggia, one including a view of the tennis courts. Yet, as much as she loved her castle and her life on the river, by the mid-1920s, there were rumors that Marjorie might also be considering adding a new love to her life. (KH.)

Four

THE TOWERS
THE THAYER YEARS

DARK ISLAND IS LOCATED IN THE LOWER SECTION OF THE ISLANDS AND IS THE SUMMER HOME OF
MRS. ALFRED THAYER

In 1926, Marjorie married Alexander D. Thayer (1888–1968), with whom she would spend the next 35 years at the Towers.

Alexander (Alec) Thayer, son of Brig. Gen. Russell Thayer and Mary Dixon of Philadelphia, was described as a dashing and attractive man. He had been the quarterback of the football team at the University of Pennsylvania. He also won several national tennis championships. In 1917, he enlisted in the military and served as an aviation instructor during World War I. He was working as an insurance stockbroker when they married. (KH.)

By October 1926, rumors were rampant that Marjorie was engaged to Alec. Marjorie adamantly denied it, proclaiming, "There is no truth to the report. I can't imagine who started the rumor. I have known Mr. Thayer a long time and we are friends." Marjorie and Alec are pictured with Marjorie's nephew, Peter Strassburger on left. (KH.)

The engagement was formally announced on November 28, 1926, and the couple was married on December 4, 1926, at the Episcopal Church of the Messiah in Gwynedd Valley, Pennsylvania. The marriage, according to one reporter, marked the culmination of a romance of long standing. It was recorded that the couple received a surprise financial bequest that had been included in her father, Frederick Bourne's will in case his youngest daughter were ever to marry.

In 1930, the Thayers purchased Gwynllan Farm, directly across from Normandy Farm, which was owned by Marjorie's sister May and her husband, Ralph Beaver Strassburger. Both properties were considered gentlemen's farms and were stocked with prized cattle cared for by a hired expert farm manager and dairy herdsman. Marjorie also raised prize German shepherds at their Gwynllan Farm Kennels.

The Thayers continued to spend their summers at the Towers on Dark Island. Pictured again is the *Dark Island*, docked at the outer slip. (KH.)

And of course Marjorie and her national champion tennis-playing husband continued to enjoy playing tennis together there on their island court. One has to wonder who won. (KH.)

Marjorie had some of her own changes and additions to the castle. In 1928, she added a third-story apartment over the piazza. Pictured is the original castle prior to the addition. (KH.)

The newly added third story (on right) allowed the Thayers their own private living quarters that were somewhat removed from the rest of the bedrooms on the island. This would give them a little extra privacy when they had overnight guests.

The second-floor apartment was composed of a suite of rooms that included the master bedroom and a sports therapy room. The sports therapy room contained an electric light bath cabinet. It is one of only three existing cabinets in existence today and is featured in every standard Singer Castle tour.

The original piazza or sun parlor below the apartment was reconstructed in stone and was divided into two separate rooms separating the original wicker room from a cozy enclosed living room with a fireplace.

For the athletic Alec's birthday in 1928, Marjorie had a squash court built on the northern side of the island. At some point the entire island was also hooked up with a sprinkler system for the tennis courts.

The squash court is in excellent condition today and is available for use by overnight guests (though the new owners and their guests prefer ping-pong over squash).

The Thayers also owned a number of boats, several of which they kept at Dark Island, including five motor boats—the *Dark Island, Wanderer, Pilot, Moike,* and *Express.* In addition, they also owned three rowing skiffs and two canoes. Pictured is one of Marjorie's postcards, showcasing the south boathouse.

In addition to their castle boat collection, the Thayers had several other yachts they kept elsewhere. This included a steel, diesel engine, 186-foot yacht they commissioned to be built in Germany in 1931, which they named the *Queen Anne.* In 1941, it was sold to the U.S. Navy, who renamed it the *Sardonyx* and placed it on U.S. shore patrol. (KH.)

The Thayers also owned the *North Star* (pictured here)—the 170-foot sister ship to the *Lone Star*, which was commissioned by Marjorie's brother George in 1928. The *Lone Star* was an entirely original new diesel yacht custom designed by Cox and Stevens. (KH.)

The Thayers owned an additional yacht named the *Antares* that they most likely kept at their winter home in Florida. (KH.)

In 1935, George Bourne (left), Alfred Bourne (center), and Alec Thayer (right) each purchased their own 16-foot GarWood boat. In 1934, GarWood received a personal request from Edward Noble (Lifesaver Candy Company) to create a small, sporty racer. Noble fell in love with the Speedster, and the first dozen produced were sent to the St. Lawrence River for him and his friends to purchase. (Anne Louise Bourne Rose.)

Alec's *Miss Chief* was eventually purchased by country music star Alan Jackson, who recently put it up for sale at the Antique Boat Show in Clayton. Noble's *Miss Step*, now known as *Miss Behave*, is a part of the museum's collection today.

In 1961, Marjorie deeded the castle to the LaSalle Christian Brothers for $1 on the condition that she could stay there until her death. Marjorie and Alec enjoyed their Towers together every summer for 36 years up until Marjorie's death in 1962. (KH.)

After Marjorie's death, it is doubtful that Alec ever returned to the castle, since she had deeded it to the LaSalle Christian Brothers. Two years later, Alec married Marjorie's sister Florence, who was also now single. Florence and Alec (pictured) were married for six years up until his death in 1968. Marjorie and Alec were buried together at the church where they were married in Gwynedd. (KH.)

Their inscription reads: "O Lord, support us all the day long of this troublesome life, until the shadows lengthen, and the evening comes, and the busy world is hushed, and the fever of life is over, and our work is done. Then, in thy great mercy, grant us a safe lodging, and a holy rest, and peace at the last, through Jesus Christ. Amen."

Though the LaSalle Christian Brothers had accepted Marjorie's generous gift, once they had taken possession of it, they found little use for a seasonal castle in the Thousand Islands. For the next three years, the castle doors remained closed.

Five

JORSTADT CASTLE
THE PREACHER AND THE SINGER

In 1965, Dr. Harold George Martin and his wife, Eloise Martin, purchased the castle on Dark Island through their ministry, the Harold Martin Evangelistic Association from Quebec, Canada for $35,000.

One of the first things the Martins did was to change the name of the castle. They called it "Jorstadt Castle" after Dr. Martin's Norwegian grandfather Olaf Jorstadt-Martin, who had been a sea captain.

The doors of the castle swung open once again. However, for the first time in its history, they were opened to the public.

Harold George Martin was a former chaplain in the Canadian Royal Air Force. He had also worked for nine years as a prison chaplain. He was a graduate of Moody Bible College and was involved in numerous ministries in Canada, including as the director of Christian Homes, the Quebec Gospel Fellowship, Christ College and Seminary, and founder of the Bethany Hope Chapel in Montreal. (RB.)

From My Heart To Yours

A personal message from
Rev. Harold Geo. Martin, Ph.D., D.D., Founder
CHRISTIAN HOMES FOR CHILDREN, INC.,
CHRIST COLLEGE AND SEMINARY
QUEBEC GOSPEL FELLOWSHIP

Beloved in Christ:
Almost ten years ago God in His wisdom brought into reality CHRISTIAN HOMES FOR CHILDREN in America, Canada and India. He has also led in the formation of the QUEBEC GOSPEL FELLOWSHIP which has over 2,000 members. Now, CHRIST COLLEGE AND SEMINARY (with accommodation for 300 students) has been organized at Hornell, N.Y. The Evening School classes have already been started and (D.V.) Day School classes will start next September. Plans are being made for a Correspondence School for those unable to attend daytime or evening classes.
There is much to report. I do hope you will take time to carefully peruse the pages of HOME magazine and pray for us and, as God has prospered you, support with your tithes and offerings this outstanding Faith Missionary Organization with its many and varied ministries.
Our work is with individual lives — Christ centered and child centered. The youth of today are the leaders of tomorrow.
To maintain a small family of five in these days of soaring costs is a problem, but to support the large

(continued inside back cover)

HOME

VIRGINIA ELOISE DORSEY MARTIN

10 cents
SUBSCRIPTION $1.00
ANYWHERE

For many years, Dr. Martin published a monthly magazine called *Home* to report on his various ministries. The booklet also included various items of interest, encouraging meditations, and devotionals. In 1939, the main item of interest, especially to Dr. Martin, was the addition of an associate editor to *Home*. She also happened to be his new bride, Virginia Eloise Dorsey Martin.

MAGNIFICAT

Thy power is sheathed
in love;

Thy love is sheathed
in kindness;

Thy kindness sheathed
in faithfulness;

All-sufficient art Thou,
O Lord!

*Eloise Dorsey Martin,
M.A., Litt.D., F.R.G.S.*

Eloise was also a Moody Bible College graduate. She was a gifted singer who often sang on the Moody radio station. It is because of the beautiful voice he heard over the radio one night that Harold ended up meeting and marrying Eloise. He claims to have known, just hearing her voice over the radio, that he was going to marry her one day.

The castle library contains books left by its various owners over the years, including a whole section of the Martins' music books and hymnals. One of the hymnals was apparently a gift Dr. Martin gave to Eloise in anticipation of their upcoming wedding. Dated April 26, 1939, Dr. Martin signed the book to "Eloise Martin—looking forward to August 4, 1939."

Harold and Eloise Martin were married on August 4, 1939. George Beverly Shea, who is referred to today as "America's Beloved Gospel Singer," sang at their wedding. Shea later earned fame as the soloist who accompanied Billy Graham on most of his worldwide evangelistic crusades. He has had an estimated cumulative live audience of 220 million people. (RB.)

Harold and Eloise had five children. The picture includes, in order of birth, their daughter, Lucretia, and their three sons, Wycliffe, Tyndale, and Calvin. Their youngest son, Wesley, had not yet been born at the time this picture was taken. (RB.)

Shortly after they purchased the castle, the Martins ran an ad in the *Watertown Times* in August 1965, announcing that this former "playground for the rich" would now be open to the public for Sunday chapel services, followed by a tour of the castle on Dark Island. Needless to say, the public began to pour through those doors, and continued to do so for the next 37 years. (RB.)

The castle was suddenly filled with music. Throughout the summer months, Dr. Martin would preach each Sunday morning and evening, and Eloise sang. Music always played a major part of the chapel services.

Like its former owners, the Martins also made a few updates and changes to the castle. The first change they made was to turn the breakfast room into a chapel with over 100 chairs and a podium. They also brought in a baby grand piano and hymnals. It should be no surprise that the hymnal they chose to use was *Inspiring Hymns*, which was the same hymnal Dr. Martin had given to Eloise in anticipation of their wedding day. (RB.)

The other significant change that the Martins made was converting the castle to electricity. In August 1969, they had 7,100 feet of sub-marine cable brought over to the island to carry electric power. The castle had formerly been powered by generators and batteries (pictured here).

Pictured is a typical cozy evening scene in the library, which was now well lit by the electricity provided by the sub-marine cable. It also allowed one to better see whoever might decide to pop their head out of the secret passageway. (RB.)

The biggest addition the Martins added to the castle was the steady stream of guests who came through its doors throughout the summer months, filling the small chapel and often overflowing onto the outer terrace. (RB.)

In addition to the Sunday chapel services, the Martins frequently entertained missionaries and pastors, held overnight retreats, made themselves available to those with spiritual questions, and were even known to invite curious passersby to come and visit with them. Dr. Martin also performed many weddings and baptisms on the island over the years. Eloise loved to entertain and was a gracious hostess to all of the summer guests. (RB.)

The summer months brought a steady flow of guests, not just on Sundays but often throughout the week as well. Dr. Martin performed weddings and river baptisms in addition to the Sunday services. The island also became a popular place for church youth groups. Pictured here is a youth group from Ottawa, along with Dr. Martin's nephew, Ralph, on the left. (RB.)

Numerous church groups came to the island over the years. Some, especially in the later years when the Martins were older, came to help out with work weekends. Some who came to the island had very little previous boating experience (getting in and out of the boat being particularly challenging to this particular group from Syracuse).

The Martins had their own collection of boats. While their boats couldn't be compared to those of the wealthy Bourne family, they obtained one rather nice boat in a most unique way. One of the regular attendees of the chapel services, Adm. Del Farney, was so touched by Eloise's lovely singing each week that he gave her his 1930s Hutchings wood boat called the *DEL*. (RB.)

The *DEL* quickly became one of the Martins' favorite boats for transporting family and guests to and from the island, as well as for simply touring them around the islands. (RB.)

They also owned a sedan-styled Chris-Craft (pictured), a metal utility/work boat, and an ice boat that they used to cross the river in the winter. (RB.)

The three summer boats spent their off-duty hours together in the south boathouse (pictured). The iceboat was kept in the north boathouse or their property on the mainland in Chippewa Bay. (RB.)

Like its previous owners, the Martins visited their island castle on a few occasions during the winter. The castle has a unique beauty during the winter that its summer guests never get to see.

When the Martins were not in residence, the castle was looked after by year-round caretakers who went back and forth to the mainland using an iceboat once the river was completely frozen over.

Count me as one who has nothing to plead.
Heavenly Friend, I am coming without any need —
Except Thy friendship.
Lord, let me be Thy friend.

Others have walked with Thee;
Laughed, loved and talked with Thee.
Help me forget all I've sought from Thee
And show me how to become Thy friend.

Should I appear in the Father's court
STILL - a bleating, bawling sheep;
STILL - one of the Shepherd's wayward flock
He's prayed "my soul to keep"?

NO! Let me become Thy friend, dear Guide,
To commune and walk close by Thy side;
And hear Thee say, at my life's end,
"Father, THIS one became My friend."

19th October, 1984   EM
Jorstadt Castle

By the 1980s, the Martins were growing older and they began to encounter various health-related issues. Eloise, in particular, found herself confined to her castle bedroom at times. Even there, she was still a poet and musician at heart, and on one such occasion penned the above poem.

The Martins put the castle on the market but still desired to keep the services going for as long as possible, even in their absence. Arriving from his campsite each week, Harvey Jones was originally much more comfortable shuttling guests. Over the next several years, he went from being called Captain Harvey to Reverend Jones. He likes to refer to this transformation as his "tents to turrets" story.

Harvey not only ended up taking over the services for the Martins. Eventually he and his wife, Flo, would spend their entire summers living at and taking care of the castle, in addition to running the Sunday services. Harvey eventually became an ordained minister and, like Dr. Martin, was able to perform weddings as well as baptisms at the island.

Harvey led the chapel services until the castle was sold in 2002, often accompanied by Patty Wilson (later Mondore), who had not only helped the Martins out with services by playing and singing, but had grown quite close to them over the years. She married Bob Mondore in 1989, and they continued to attend the summer services together. Bob also began filming with future projects in mind.

In keeping with the castle's long-running tradition, music was an important part of each service. Harvey and Patty were both singers who sang nearly every week. It was common for many of the guests to also share special songs (pictured is the Yaiser family). Harvey also led the congregation in hymns, still using the *Inspiring Hymns* hymnal right up until the castle was sold in 2002.

Six

SINGER CASTLE

RENOVATIONS AND INVESTMENTS

In 2003, a group of investors called Dark Island Tours, Inc. purchased the aging castle and changed its name to Singer Castle. Since their initial investment, they have put almost 10 million additional dollars into the restoration and renovation of this major centerpiece of local history.

Even as the renovations were underway, it took very little time before the castle doors were reopened. Singer Castle quickly became one of the most visited new tourist attractions in the Thousand Islands area and now averages over 20,000 visitors per year. (FV.)

While the castle has several of its own boats, it also has a new fleet of vessels regularly parked at its docks. From mid-May through mid-October, tour boats bring delighted tourists to take a trip back into time and experience the wonder and history of this 100-year-old castle. What many do not realize is all of the time, effort, and investment the owners poured into the castle to make this possible. (FV.)

The years had begun to take their toll on the castle. While its owners made numerous cosmetic renovations to the castle through the years, a number of major structural repairs also needed to be made. To be able to open to the public, it needed to meet certain codes and standards. The next few pages show you highlights of the castle as it looks today, as well as some of the exquisite renovations that have brought the castle back to its original pristine condition. Tom Weldon, president of Singer Castle, also provided a look at some of the massive repair efforts, taking place behind-the-scenes to secure the castle's future. (FV.)

The first major renovation anyone will notice upon arrival is the dock. The docks at both the south and north boathouses had been almost completely eroded away and were virtually unusable. Today, guests will arrive to dock at the biggest one-piece floating dock on the St. Lawrence. Measuring 100 feet long, with 6-foot baffles, this all new dock was built for Singer Castle by TIECO Floating Docks and Marine structures, Landstowne, Ontario.

The docks have been made with 10 one-ton weights hung from 10 chains. Tom described how one of those barrels broke loose one winter. It floated down the river and conveniently ended up in Morristown at a castle employee's dock. Also note the gas tank to the right. While maintaining its original look, this castle fixture is now used as the Dark Island trash receptacle.

Guests can once again walk up the familiar bridle path and now enter the castle through its beautifully refinished front door.

If Frederick Bourne were to enter his Great Hall today he would hardly notice that any time had passed since his last visit. It has been restored to appear nearly identical to its original condition, and many of the original furnishings are still in place. What was no longer there, such as Bourne's three sets of antique armor, have historically appropriate replacements. (FV.)

Just off the great hall is the meticulously maintained library. Most of the original books remain on the shelves. In this room are many precious reminders of the castle's history and its various owners. The library today also contains some historically significant additions (see pages 20, 46, and 80). (FV.)

Just to the left of the fireplace is the panel that can be opened to reveal a hidden entrance to one of the two secret passageway systems running throughout the castle. Like most of the secret passageway entrances, it is opened through a hidden switch, this one being located in the bookcase next to the panel.

The splendidly proportioned stone stairs of the grand staircase lead to the main floor. They are flanked by the original highly polished hand-carved wooden balustrades and newel posts.

What the casual visitor would not be aware of is that there is another panel at the top of the stairs that also enters the secret passageways. The hidden switch to this entrance is cleverly located underneath the light fixture next to the panel.

One of the major renovations Dark Island Tours, Inc. invested in putting in a whole new electrical system. They completely replaced thousands of feet of old wiring with a 600-amp service running throughout the castle, and a new transformer. Pictured are three views of the original generator system located in the north boathouse, with a view of the new transformer at the right.

A new potable water system was installed in the basement of castle, as the water at the castle was required to pass a strict test for purity. Two samples were taken to an independent lab, and not only did the potable water system pass with flying colors, but the water sample taken directly from the river's deep waters also passed the test.

The magnificent trophy room looks strikingly similar to the way it did 100 years earlier, complete with the original game trophies adoring its walls (see page 24). (FV.)

The large portrait of King Charles II overlooking the room can be pulled open from inside one of the passageways so that the entire room can be observed from above (note the painting is tilted slightly open). Note also that despite some rumors to the contrary, Charles's eyes do not move.

While touring the islands, the maidens and knights who come to visit will all appreciate the investment made in a complete wastewater treatment system. These new facilities are located behind the billiard room in what was formerly used as Bourne's storage room (see page 21).

All of this is possible because of a modern wastewater treatment system installed in the former icehouse that takes wastewater and releases it back into river in a state that is purer than the river itself. The system handles up to 5,000 gallons of water per week.

Here is a peek at Frederick Bourne's turret office, located in the south corner of the trophy room. The round office has been restored with original furnishings, including Frederick Bourne's personal safe. Also of note is the antler chandelier, which was designed with a combination of gas and electric power.

Pictured here is the formal dining room. The table is the original A. J. Horner table used by the Bourne family (see page 24). The small square grid on the upper center of the wall is one of the places where those in the secret passageways can peer down into the room below.

Just beyond the dining room is the breakfast room. Dark Island Tours, Inc. transformed this room from the Martins' chapel back to its original use. Today, overnight guests have their option of taking meals in either the dining room or the breakfast room.

The Martins frequently used the terrace off of the breakfast room during chapel services. However, at the time Dark Island Tours, Inc. purchased the castle, the entire structure was in danger of collapsing. It took a major investment of time, labor, and money to restore this section of the castle.

Also on this floor are the loggia (see page 70) and the wicker room. The piano pictured here was formerly used for the Sunday services in the chapel. It was donated by one of the Martins' sons, who was an accomplished pianist. Overnight guests are free to play and sing to their hearts' content.

Pictured here is the bedroom at the end of Marjorie's third-story suite of rooms. The suite also includes the sports therapy room with its electric light bath cabin, among other unique and original furnishings (see page 70).

One of the most luxuriously restored areas in the castle is the Royal Suite. The Royal Suite is one wing of the castle with two bedrooms and a bath. It is not a part of the standard tour but is reserved exclusively for overnight guests from May 1 to November 1. In addition to enjoying the run of the castle for the night, visitors experience the wonder of the magnificent three-sided river views from their private suite.

There are two elegantly decorated bedrooms, a fully modernized bathroom, baseboard electric heat, and wireless Internet access. Among other things, the Royal Suite makes a perfect honeymoon suite.

Dr. Martin and Harvey Jones both performed numerous weddings during the Martin years. Singer Castle continues that tradition today, averaging 10–12 weddings per year. Weddings are held in various locations on the castle grounds, including the lovely rose garden on the south side of the island. The caretaker's cottage has been converted to a bridal house where the bridal party can dress, prepare, and then enter the ceremony. Weddings, of course, often include singers and other musicians. (Both, FV.)

One of the fun new features one can discover on a tour of Singer Castle is the wonderful collection of antique sewing machines (all Singer, of course), located throughout the castle. Each machine, dating from as far back as 1894, was donated to the castle. Most are from the time of Frederick Bourne.

The oldest machine received to date came from Myron Sierson, who determined that the castle would be the perfect place for the antique sewing machines his grandmother and mother had used. Sierson's grandmother, Bertha Cusworth, used an 1894 treadle machine with cabinet until the early 1970s.

Another donation to the castle is a magnificent Frederick Remington sculpture displayed on the fireplace mantel in the dining room. The sculpture is on loan from the Frederick Remington Museum in nearby Ogdensburg, New York. Remington had an island (Ingleneuk Island) just across the river from Frederick Bourne, and legend has it that he was not overly pleased at seeing a castle being constructed so close to his private retreat.

Of course no tour is complete without a stop at the clock tower. The clock tower was added as a fifth-floor addition somewhere between 1911 and 1916. The clock itself is an E. Howard clock and has a set of Westminster chimes designed to play on the quarter-hour.

Today the clock continues to chime every 15 minutes throughout the summer months, as clearly and reliably as the day it was made. This is thanks in part to the meticulous care it receives from the island caretaker, Scott Garris.

While the castle may close to the public in mid-October, it remains occupied year-round by its caretaker, Scott Garris. Scott has the opportunity to see a side of the castle that most would not get to see, except through his photography. While he keeps busy taking care of the castle throughout the long winter months, he managed to take a little time off to capture a few of its many breathtakingly beautiful moments. (Scott Garris)

The kitchen has been fully modernized and is often full of activity, serving overnight guests or being used by caterers for weddings or other events. But even there, pieces of history remain. The owners were able to repair the original servant call box located in the outer kitchen area to the left.

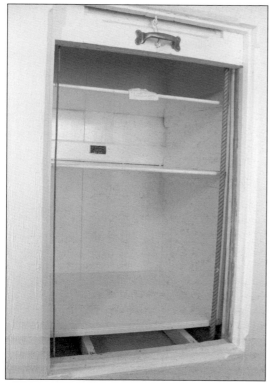

Another piece of functional history are the castle dumbwaiters. They have all been restored to perfect working order and can be used to service the dining room located directly above the kitchen. The owners have also installed a fire detection system and extinguishers throughout the castle. And for the first time in the castle's history, it now has phone service. The previous owners used a radio to communicate with the mainland.

While this short tour will not be able to stop in all 30 of its rooms, it will take a quick trip upstairs for a glimpse at the dormitory. The dormitory room features a large cathedral ceiling, windows on all four sides, and has its own turret bathroom. It was originally designed as quarters for the female servants. Today, it also contains a Singer sewing machine and a microwave dish.

Two additional bedrooms can be accessed from this level. One is a step-down room (pictured) across from the dorm room. A ladder located in a closet just outside this room goes up to the water tower turret. Going up one more flight of winding stone stairs, one arrives at the top-floor map or tower room. This room might have originally only been accessible through secret passageways.

One of the most fascinating features of the castle are its secret passageways with their many intriguing hidden entrances. There are actually two separate passageway systems. One system is five stories tall and was designed so servants could go discreetly from the ground level to the upper bedrooms. This first system also includes the passageways that lead to portrait of King Charles II, as well as the dungeon located in the turret.

There are two sets of spiral staircases found in the castle's passageways. The second passageway system is three stories tall and runs from north boathouse underground (underneath the back lawn) to the castle, the clock tower, and ultimately to the south boathouse.

The south boathouse is the perfect place to end this tour, because today it also serves, in part, as the castle gift shop (where visitors can pick up historical souvenirs as well as extra copies of *Singer Castle* or *Singer Castle Revisited*).

Though the owners have already invested millions of dollars into their castle, they are in no way finished with all of what they hope to be able to do. One of their future projects is to repair and renovate the north boathouse. Perhaps they will even be able to find out what happened to the guy who left his boots in the furnace.

In the meantime, they have already made a major investment in the north boathouse by putting a temporary roof on the building to prevent any further damage. The dream is to repair the structure and renovate the insides so that this, too, becomes a part of the wonder of Singer Castle.

Seven

SINGER CASTLE

FACES AND FINAL REFLECTIONS

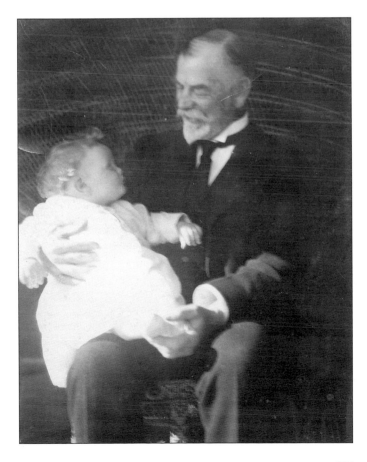

This return visit to Singer Castle will end with a last look at the faces of those who made, and are making, the castle what it is today. Pictured here is Frederick Bourne enjoying time with one of his many grandchildren. (KH.)

Of course the first faces to would have to be Frederick (1851–1919) and Emma (1855–1916) Bourne. Marjorie's *Dark Island* book reads, "To his surviving children, no dearer memory remains than that of the hours the family spent with him and Mrs. Bourne singing." This generous and kind-hearted couple would no doubt be pleased to know how many others are enjoying their Singer Castle today. (KH.)

Marjorie Bourne (1890–1962), also fondly referred to as "Hooley," owned the castle from 1921 to 1962. It is partly thanks to her generosity in deeding it to the Christian Brothers that it ended up in the hands of its present owners today. Marjorie married Alexander Thayer in 1926, and they shared the Towers up until her death in 1962. Pictured is Marjorie in her trophy–winning speedboat, the *Moike*. (KH)

Harold and Eloise Martin, under the name of their Harold Martin Evangelistic Association ministry, owned the castle they renamed Jorstadt from 1965 until Dark Island Tours, Inc. purchased it in 2002. It is because of the vision they had for using it to share their faith with others that the castle doors were opened for the first time to the public. (RB.)

When they were no longer able come to the island, much less to continue the weekly services, it was thanks to Harvey and Flo Jones that the castle doors were able to remain open for several more years. The chapel services continued up until the castle's sale in 2002. (Harvey Jones.)

The entire staff at Singer Castle is remarkable. This project could not have been completed without the help of castle historian Judy Keeler (second from right). Tom Weldon (second from left) is president of Singer Castle, overseeing its daily affairs and keeping it running smoothly. Also pictured are administrative assistant Jean Papke (right) and operations manager Pam Thomas (left).

One might say it takes a village to run a castle. But it takes an extremely talented and dedicated staff to run Singer Castle. The picture includes some of the summer tour guides, Judy, Pam, Jean, as well as caretaker, Scott Garris, who is pictured in the center of the second row.

Before there was a Singer Castle, Patty Mondore was the castle singer. On a recent return visit she found her old friend, the piano, now residing in the sun parlor. The Mondores are the authors of both *Singer Castle* and *Singer Castle Revisited*.

Bob Mondore is also the author of the popular Singer Castle blog (singercastle.blogspot.com) where he continually blogs the latest news and other interesting stories about Singer Castle and the Thousand Islands area.

Also on staff at Singer Castle are a couple of other familiar faces. Harvey and Flo Jones represented the castle at an event held by the Hammond Historical Society. Harvey also moonlights on occasion as an official castle tour guide.

While Ken Hard and his wife, Christel, have never actually been able to visit the castle, they have become a vital part of its history. Ken is the grandson of Frederick Bourne and has also taken it upon himself to be one of the family's most faithful historians. It is because of his willingness to share the Bourne family's marvelous collection of photographs that this book was possible. Hopefully he and Christel can come and visit in person some day. (KH.)

Ralph Berry is the nephew of Harold and Eloise Martin and spent many summers visiting them at the castle. Many of the pictures in this book were from Ralph, who recently brought his daughters to visit the castle.

Since Ralph's wife, Miriam, was not able come, he called her from the very Pullman seat in the trophy room where he had proposed to her 20 years earlier (she said yes).

PREFACE

Because Dark Island and the majestic river in which it rests are so beautiful, and because it is all so different, visitors find much to excite their interest.

It was therefore quite natural that the suggestion should occur to Miss Bourne that a volume describing in brief form something of the island and the surrounding territory would make a memento of the visits of her friends which they would appreciate.

It was further suggested that a short biographical sketch of Commodore Bourne, who built "The Towers," would be a fitting theme to incorporate in such a volume.

The task of compiling the story seemed to provide a most effective way for me to express my appreciation for the opportunities that came to me to visit Dark Island. But rather it has been a pleasure, as it has made me know the place and its surroundings better.

And if the story answers some of your questions and in that way adds even a little to the enjoyment of your visit, it will have served its purpose.

H. D. B.

Yet another individual who has played an important role in the castle's history is the mysterious H. D. B., who wrote and published the *Dark Island* book some time in the early 1920s for Marjorie Bourne. The preface he wrote back then could have just been as appropriately written by the authors of *Singer Castle Revisited* today.

And then, of course, there is Fred. Other than Scott, Fred is the only other year-round resident of the island. Currently located in the dungeon, he is most likely not one of the castle's original guests, despite the cobwebs indicating he (or she) has been there for some time. Only overnight guests have the privilege of meeting him in person, face to . . . skull.

It is only because of their vision and the many millions of dollars invested by Dark Island Tours, Inc. that the castle has become the major historical landmark it is today. This aerial photograph, taken by Farhad Vladi, is to represent the three owners, and to let them know how much their investments have meant to all who have had the pleasure of experiencing the wonder of Singer Castle. (FV.)

The last faces that play an important part in the history of the castle on Dark Island are those of the many individuals who have come through its doors to experience the wonder of Singer Castle for themselves. In so doing, they too, have stepped into its history. (TV.)

The history of Singer Castle is not over yet. In fact, it is only just beginning. Even as guests continue to flow through its doors, renovations are continually underway behind the scenes. Everyone who makes the trip across the mighty St. Lawrence Seaway to visit the castle on Dark Island becomes a part of its history, no matter what kind of boat one uses to get there.

Discover Thousands of Local History Books
Featuring Millions of Vintage Images

Arcadia Publishing, the leading local history publisher in the United States, is committed to making history accessible and meaningful through publishing books that celebrate and preserve the heritage of America's people and places.

Find more books like this at
www.arcadiapublishing.com

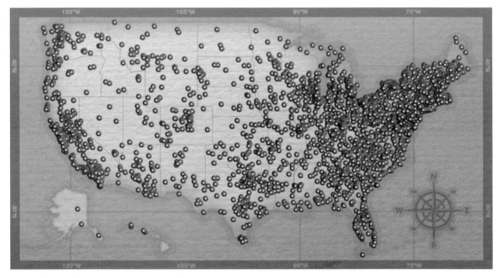

Search for your hometown history, your old stomping grounds, and even your favorite sports team.